Words and WONDER

A GUIDE TO BECOMING A CREAT...

Ipsum

DANA DE GREFF

AUTHOR OF ALTERATIONS
WINNER OF THE RANE ARROYO CHAPBOOK SERIES

Print ISBN: 978-1-66782-493-2
eBook ISBN: 978-1-66782-494-9

Printed in the United States of America

TABLE OF CONTENTS

INTRODUCTION

BEFORE I WAS a writer, I was a reader. I was happy to spend hours reading *Nancy Drew*, *Encyclopedia Brown*, and *Goosebumps*. In middle school I was on the *Harry Potter* train and obsessed with Holocaust survival accounts (one part heritage, one part exhilaration, and a dash of morbidity at twelve years old). But it wasn't until high school that I read a book, *Beloved* by Toni Morrison, leaned back and thought: *This. This is what I want to do.* She set a very, very high bar. (And thanks to my English teacher, Ms. Simmons, for this positive obsession.)

Since the age of sixteen, there have been many roadblocks, traffic jams, holes, bear attacks, getting stuck in the mud, hallucinations, deviations, and just being utterly and completely lost along the way to my path of becoming a writer. I studied creative writing as an undergrad and then I went to Spain, fell in love, drank a lot of wine and ate a lot of cheese. I came back to the US, got a Master's in Creative Writing, fell in love again, read a lot, wrote a lot, then got hit with the recession and self-doubt. Then I went to Iowa City and read and wrote a lot and made a lot of mistakes, followed by 14 months in Patagonia (you'll have to wait for the memoir to get all the details on that).

Finally, I came back to Miami in 2013 and began working as an editor for a publication/media company. Okay, you might be thinking, *that's* when she became a writer. And it makes sense…I was writing, reading, editing, and researching every day. But it wasn't for my stories, or poetry, or books. No, it was for diamonds, trips to Bimini, and special spa services, products for people I would never meet. It was a formula, it was tedious, and I quickly grew miserable. By the time I got home, the last thing I wanted to do was write. So, I did everything and anything else: Netflix, bars, clubs, dating, travel, parties. Looking back, I don't think I was very happy in my late twenties. And much of that is because I had given up on my dream of becoming a writer.

~ ◆ ~

In 2015, I made a big decision and applied for a Master's in Fine Arts in Creative Writing at two programs: the University of Iowa Writers' Workshop (the crème de la crème) and the University of Miami (good, but no Carver's or Chandler's graduated from there). I didn't get into Iowa, but I did get into UM, and those three years changed my life.

Just to be clear, though, this book will not be a treatise on why you should get an MFA. For some people, like me, it saved my writing because it gave me time and forced me to make big changes in order to make writing a priority in my life again. For others, the MFA program model is counterproductive and even harmful. I'll get into that later. Point is, from the time I said "I want to do that" to doing the damn thing, more than ten years had passed.

In other words, if you're in the same boat as I was, and you know you want out, or you know you want to make writing a priority in your life, I'm here to say this: there's time. But you must start now.

I hope this book—and the bits and pieces I've learned about writing and the writing life—helps.

P.S. Throughout the book I will provide you with various "De Greff Doors" which are prompts meant to get you thinking, creating, and, of course, writing.

P.P.S. If you have a hard copy, feel free to write all over this work. If not, get a fresh notebook (delight!) and dedicate it to all the prompts and musings found here.

ONE

WHY YOU SHOULD WRITE

I'LL BE HONEST with you: there is no reason you 'should' do anything, in my opinion, outside of take care of yourself and your loved ones with food, clothing, housing, education, health, care, and love. That's already a lot in this world. But, if you *love* writing, if you *love* reading, then yes, you *should* write, because a life well lived does, ideally, go beyond basic human needs. We're wired for a desire for art and expression and creativity. Those of us who don't create art most certainly consume it, and if you're reading this book, odds are you're a creator in some shape or form.

Revision: I can't really say why you should write (or do anything), but I can tell you why I do. I write because I want to share my stories with others, even if I never get to meet them, even if you, dear reader, living and breathing on the other side of this screen, or with a physical copy in your hands, are someone I can't physically see or touch. Perhaps that is what makes this even more magical. To know we are in conversation via signs and symbols on the page, and that I may, just maybe, offer you a glimmer of delight, a glimmer of possibility. I also write because I consider books to be my friends and family, and to better understand the world.

Another revision: Perhaps why you should write isn't the right question. Because it's not about convincing you or getting you to come to the dark (but quite rewarding) side. It's a choice. You need to *choose* to write, to become a writer, every day. It's a progression, it's a river with many ebbs and flows, it has no straight line. Some days, the choice is easy, and you just do it. Some days, it's torturous, and you'd rather go to the dentist. But if you truly want to write, then you must choose it. Give yourself permission to choose what you love and what you fear. (Both of those are good indications that it's the right choice, by the way.) And if you're not ready to believe that you can choose, then listen to me: you can, and you can start today. Right now.

But first, it's important to know why you will choose to come back to the page again and again, why the rejections and doubt will be worth this choice, why showing up for yourself and your writing every day will be worth it. To help you get to the bottom of this, you'll need to do some brainstorming…

DE GREFF DOOR #1

Take some time to brainstorm and journal on the following questions. Don't hold back. These answers are just for you, but I suggest you write them in your journal, as well as on a notecard that you can tape to your wall, or above the place you write, or on a mirror, somewhere easy to view and that may serve as a constant reminder of your choice to write and to be a writer.

1. Why do you want to write?

2. What has stopped you in the past?

3. What drives you to write now?

4. Why will you make the choice to write now, tomorrow, and beyond?

TWO

BEATING IMPOSTER SYNDROME

BEFORE GETTING INTO the meat of imposter syndrome, I want to take a moment to be as transparent and open as possible. On paper, I know I have a lot going on when it comes to writing: I have an MA from the University of Texas, an MFA in Creative Writing from the University of Miami, I've published a poetry chapbook that won a prize, I've been awarded thousands of dollars in funding and scholarships for my writing-in-progress, had residencies in the woods of Georgia and a chalet in Tuscany, been nominated for a Pushcart Prize, and written (but not yet published) two novels.

I don't say all of this to brag, but rather, to explain that despite these accolades, despite this outward success, I, too, still struggle with imposter syndrome. For me, this topic is very personal, and if I can help anyone else work through it and come out stronger and freer creatively, then I know I'll have done my part. In my humble opinion, there is nothing more difficult, but also nothing more exhilarating, than writing. And in my 10+ years of teaching writing and leading workshops for all ages, from six years old to eighty, one of the biggest hindrances that gets in the way of finishing a book, story, poem, blog post, etc., is the writer themselves.

We tend to give in to our anxieties, fears, and (false) beliefs that what we're writing is just not "good enough" or that we're not talented enough or qualified enough to write whatever we're working on. But the thing is, it's simply not true. Beliefs are not facts, but rather, narratives we tell ourselves. The good news is, if you've ever felt any of this before, you're not alone. Imposter syndrome, or what psychologists call 'imposter phenomenon,' is experienced by 70% of people at some point in their lives according to a 2018 article in the *International Journal of Behavioral Science.*

The idea that you may have succeeded due to luck and not because of talent or qualifications is something many of us feel, and certainly not just writers. Human beings often internalize ideas they learned at a young age. You might, for example, struggle with confidence in other areas of your life, and so it's natural that this would affect how you think about your writing. You might believe writing a book, story, or even an "About

Me" page is such an uphill battle, such a daunting task, why even bother doing it?

Believe me, I get it. Not only do I get it, but I've also done it. I've had many conversations with myself over the last few years about whether this writing thing is a crapshoot, a pipe dream, a crazy fantasy, or delusions of grandeur. I've told myself my writing is garbage, and nobody will ever publish or read it. I've told myself that I am a masochist because why else would I go into a career where 'no' is the common response and books are published based on taste and what's en vogue, and there is no formula for taste or trends. Give it up, I've told myself. Your life will be so much easier.

At the end of the day, these thoughts will come. Unless you're an enlightened being who has everything figured out and remains nonplussed by rejection, never feels a shred of doubt, and loves every single thing that you do, think, say, and feel, it's going to happen. The real trick then, is what to do when these feelings and thoughts arise.

Here is what I suggest: write down your negative thoughts and feelings, acknowledge them, and then move on to something else. Or write them down and then you can vent these feelings and thoughts to a close friend who can offer support (ideally a fellow writer) or send them to me in a longwinded email that I probably won't reply to. The simple act of sending your concerns to someone else does wonders.

If you're not comfortable venting out loud to people, I've also tried a technique called 'conscious complaining' which I learned about from Karla McLaren's book *The Language of Emotions: What Your Feelings Are Trying to Tell You*, in which she suggests you vent your grievances out to the trees on a long walk as a means of release. Life is unfair! I've shouted to the coconut palms. Writing is so hard, I say to the oaks. I just got another rejection, can you believe this shit, I ask the banyans. They always shake their leaves in understanding at the injustice of it all because they're always on my side—it's quite cathartic.

Another thing that helps me that you can also try is to remind yourself that your beliefs may not be (read: are probably not) based in reality. Ergo, if you *feel* like an imposter, that doesn't mean you *are* one. And guess what? Famous writers deal with this all the time, even great talents like Maya Angelou. She famously said, "Each time I write a book, every time I face that yellow pad, the challenge is so great. I have written eleven books, but each time I think, 'Uh oh, they're going to find out now. I've run a game on everybody and they're going to find me out.'"

The real danger of imposter syndrome is that it can cause procrastination for a writer, or worse, make you give up writing altogether. So do everything you can to challenge those thoughts when they arise. And when it comes to your writing, one of the best tips I can impart is to give yourself permission to suck, or as Brené Brown says, "embrace the suck." Actually, I'll take it one step further: I say embrace the shit. Write shitty words and shitty sentences and shitty drafts. This will take the pressure off you and allow you to lean into the messy, fun, and liberating joy that is creating art.

Remember, it's supposed to be shitty in the beginning. It's supposed to be wild and nonsensical. We're not going for perfectionism, because perfectionism is the death of art. We're going for well-crafted sentences and books, but you don't get that from nothing. You get that from something, and more times than not, it begins with shit. (Note: For a great essay on writing shit, read Anne Lammot's "Shitty First Drafts.")

DE GREFF DOOR #2

Brainstorm and journal on the following questions:

1. What scares me the most about writing?

2. What has stopped me from reaching my goal of writing (insert project) thus far?

3. Why do I write, or why do I want to write?

4. What is one positive, optimistic phrase I can tell myself when I'm feeling down, or discouraged, or fearful about writing? (For example, mine is: I am a writer, no matter what happens. My stories matter. The world needs my stories.)

THREE

HOW TO FIND INSPIRATION

"To be able to face our fears, we must remember how to per-
form ritual. To remember how to perform ritual, we must slow
down."—Malidoma Somé

THERE ARE MANY ways to find inspiration, and many people will have different answers for this. But there are some tried
and true methods that have worked for me, and ideally, you'll
find inspiration from my inspiration, share your findings with
other writers, and continue the cycle. Because I think the first
trick to finding inspiration is finding someone you can share
what inspires you with. This can be a fellow writer, an online
community, a friend, family, a tree, or a pet. There's something
about speaking it out loud that makes it more powerful.

So here is a list, in no particular order, of what inspires me:

13

1. Reading (if you don't read you should be reading everything you can get your hands on starting now);

2. Music (and making playlists for my projects, a very fun way to match sound to the visuals you are creating);

3. Dance (I was a tango student for a couple of years, and the ability to get out of my head and into my body was key, especially when I was feeling stuck or unmotivated);

4. Film (a great film can get me ready to create, especially as someone who once had a dream to be a famous screenwriter…working on it!);

5. Art (same as above, especially since I am a visual person at heart);

6. Breathing. I often use the 4-4-5 technique (inhale for four counts, hold for four counts, exhale for five counts, and repeat), which helps reduce stress, let go of the day, and fully arrive to the writing ready to create; also, to get scientific, this sort of breathing technique helps stimulate the parasympathetic nerve, which controls our rest state, and deactivates the sympathetic nervous system which regulates our fight-or-flight response, allowing for a better head space for writing;

7. Journaling (this can be on anything, really: words, dreams, plants, history...for a truly wonderful and thorough list of journal ideas, google "Bernadette Mayer's Writing Experiments" and go wild);

8. Nature, or any place I can be away from the city and people being loud and obnoxious (people can be loud and obnoxious outside, but it's not as grating);

9. Travel (since 2020 certainly not an ideal time for this, but there is also armchair travel, which allows one to go to any place in the world via a book, film, documentary, show, podcast...all for free, or very cheap!);

10. Research. I know, very nerdy, but when I need to be inspired, I allow and encourage myself to go down the rabbit hole, which has led me to learn a ton about things like Patagonian flora, Japanese whiskey, Roberto Clemente...

11. Other writers, especially those I admire, and think are doing great work on and off the page. I listen to podcasts, go to readings, read craft essays, and more to get a boost of inspo when needed;

12. My writer friends. When I'm feeling sorry for myself, or down on my art, or writing in general, I reach out to them for words of support, or just to vent. And it's

quite lovely to be understood. If you don't have writer friends, now is the time to find one. All you need is one. And if you're lost on where to start, try a writer's meetup, or join my Writing Circle. I write with other writers twice a week, every week via zoom, and the support helps, as well as seeing others doing the thing;

13. Come up with writing rituals. They help set the mood, get you into the flow state, and treat writing as a sacred activity. When I use the word 'sacred' I simply mean writing is sacred insofar as it's important to you and is a large part of your life, and therefore deserving of time, care, and reverence. Some of my rituals include making a cup of tea, lighting a candle, writing down my goals in my current notebook, meditating, etc.

14. Write a personal manifestation for why you are writing, or what you are writing.

DE GREFF DOOR #3

To get you started on your journey to inspiration, your challenge here is to write your own writing manifesto. Here are the ingredients I think are necessary for a powerful manifestation:

1. Be as specific (but also realistic—nobody can write a novel in a week, for example, or get a trillion-dollar book deal) as possible;

2. Form is not so important here, so be creative as you like and make this a poem, an essay, bullet points, stars, collage, whatever you want but it MUST have words;

3. Ask for aid from another source if that makes sense to you, such as the universe, Buddha, your ancestors,

Ala, other authors, anyone or any being that gives you a sense of strength/courage/possibility;

4. Say thank you at the end, be grateful and trust in all that will come, and remember to return to this often. You may even want to include it in your meditation practice.

FOUR

HOW TO FIND TIME TO WRITE/ HOW TO WRITE THROUGH FEAR

AS AN EDUCATOR, coach, and mentor, one of the most frequent questions I get from emerging writers is: How do I find the time to write? I have work, kids, stress, health issues, no motivation, no money…the list goes on. And we get creative with our excuses, too. Some of the most common ones I've heard are:

1. "I was so busy today/this week I just didn't have time…"

2. "I'll do it next week when I'm more organized…"

3. "I'll start writing when I'm motivated…"

4. "I'll get to it once I quit my day job and have more time…"

5. "Nobody will read my work anyway so what's the point?"

Here's the thing: there is no perfect time or moment to write. I've been in the woods in Georgia, literally being paid to write, and found excuses not to that had nothing to do with time. It was all mental, and I believe that we often get in our own heads and find ways to not write. There will always be a hindrance, an inconvenience, a story. The trick is, then, to find tools and techniques to work around these excuses. We need to find ways to just get the words down, and you may need to experiment a lot to figure out what works best for you.

Note: this is not to say that life doesn't get in the way, because I know it does. Sometimes, yes, we are primary care-givers, or ill, or in survival mode just trying to pay rent and eat. And when that happens, I suggest you simply be kind to yourself and remember that writing happens even when you're not writing. You can think about your writing, plan in your mind, or on scraps of paper, and when you can come back to the page, trust that you'll be ready to go.

Underneath the other excuses, however, I think what may be lurking is fear. Fear of failure, fear of inadequacy, fear of being an imposter, fear of not being good enough, fear of not knowing enough, fear of disappointing people, fear of not getting published, fear of getting published and getting slammed by the press, fear of dying before anything ever goes to print…I could go on, but I won't. Point is, fear, and not time, is often what is blocking us from writing.

If this applies to you, I want you to write one of your fears associated with writing, or your current project, down on paper. Next, I'd like you to pretend that you're writing a letter to that fear or having a conversation with it. For example:

Dear fear of not getting your book published,

First of all, I hear you. So much work and time has gone into you and you just want to be seen! That is so real, and I feel you. However, editors are reading you right now. You have to be patient. And if they say no, which is quite possible, it doesn't mean you're shit. It just means now is not the right time for you to come out in the world. But I believe there will be a right time, and so should you.

Love,

Dana

By naming the fear (s), you can start to tame them, and maybe even learn from them. Because fear can either ruin your life or enhance it. Fear will never go away, but we can choose to use it for our growth as opposed to our destruction, and the following are some tips/techniques to help you get past the fear, as well as create and choose to give yourself more time to write:

1. Develop a writing habit/discipline. Something I have recently found out about habits, which kind of blew my mind, is that the magic number of 21 days to form a habit is just a myth. I don't know how long it takes to form a habit, but I think it's important to keep in mind that everyone is different. Some of us are pretty good at time management, discipline, and deadlines, and some of us aren't, but I do think we can all improve the more we have the right intention and actions in place. It's not enough to say you want to do something, then write down a schedule and goals; you can't stop there, you must also follow through and take action.

What works best for me is having times of day to write that I show up to consistently. This may take some trial and error, but try and figure out when you work best: early morning? Afternoon? Night? Before work? After work? Weekends? My sweet spot seems to be before lunch and from 5-7 pm, thanks to my awesome writing circle, and on the weekends after some outdoor walking or yoga, anything that activates my parasympathetic nerve.

I will say that for most people, writing after work is hard, so if you can, wake up earlier and do it before work. This is nice too if you live with other people, because as they sleep you can get shit done and have precious quiet time. Even 30 minutes a day makes a difference.

2. If you can't get up earlier, try and write in those moments during the day when you have small breaks, such as during your commute (if you ride public transportation, always have a notebook with you) or lunch break. If you're working at home like me, then you can 'take a lunch break' and go to another room, or a café, or outside, or even your car. Just form the habit of when I eat, I write, or when I travel, I write. It will start to feel like second nature eventually.

3. TURN. OFF. THE. PHONE. Seriously, just having it in the room with you is energetically distracting. Stay in the writing zone and put it in another room, lock it away, or turn it off.

4. Turn off the internet while you write on your laptop. It can be just for 20 or 30 minutes, but it helps to avoid those 'quick' little social media checks/shopping/weather views that, again, take us out of the writing zone.

5. When you come home from work and you want to write but are drained or tired, try taking a short walk first. Get fresh air, sweat, and then go to the computer or notebook, sans phone. It's a great way to leave the day behind.

6. Same as above, but try the 4-4-5 breathing technique before you write, or listen to a guided meditation. I recently

tried a 5-minute one specifically for writers led by Kimine Mayuzumi that helped a lot.

7. Read. If I'm not in the mood to write, or angry/upset/stressed, I reach for a book. Oftentimes, this allows my brain and body to relax, and I get inspired by a great line or image and then I'm ready. I have a list going on Bookshop of all my books if you need recs.

8. Block off time on your calendar for writing. By putting it in your schedule, it shows that this is a priority in your life.

9. Reward yourself when you complete a goal. Go get an ice cream, a beer, or a brand-new notebook. I love Flame Tree Journals!

DE GREFF DOOR #4

PREMEDITATIO MALORUM, OR the premeditation of evils or troubles that lie ahead, is a Stoic exercise of imagining all that could go wrong for us in life. And I know that doesn't sound very fun, but it can help us prepare for the inevitable rejection and setbacks when it comes to writing and getting your work published, especially through more traditional means. Just thinking our way through fear doesn't work—we need to write our way through it.

On that note, turn to a brand-new page in your journal and write for the next 10-15 minutes on whatever it is you fear about writing a specific piece, or writing in general. For example, here is what I came up with:

If I finish my memoir and have my agent submit it to editors, it may get a large amount of nos. But it will hurt even more this time because this is not fiction—I am writing about my life. I am scared that if I write my memoir and try and publish it, and it doesn't get published, not only am I a failed writer, I have somehow also failed at my life. And those two rejections side by side will put me in a bad place emotionally, mentally, and physically.

Now it's your turn.

Once you are done with that, you will then journal for another 10-15 minutes on what you might do if your worst fears came true, or who you could ask for help. For example:

If my memoir is rejected by all the editors it is sent to, then I can either let it go and congratulate myself for a valiant effort, or I can self-publish it. I don't have to be with a big publishing house. If I want it in the world, then I can get it out there on my own and not let taste and gatekeepers stand in my way.

Next you will journal for another 10-15 minutes, but this time think about what you might gain by writing what scares you. Here is what I came up with:

Even trying to publish my memoir is a huge move for me. Until two years ago, I only wrote fiction and poetry. I am working in a new genre and writing about hard things, but I still do it because I think my story matters, I matter, and I would rather try than wonder what if. This will give me confidence, and build self-esteem, and allow me to grow as an artist.

Now turn to another new page.

On this page, write for as long as you need to on what your life might be like if you don't write this piece, or if you don't write at all. Get really detailed. How will your life be different without writing being an essential and important element in it? This is what I wrote:

If I don't publish my memoir, then I will always wonder what if. I have already invested a year in this project, and I want to see it through. If I don't, I will know how close I was, and how I let fear rule my decisions, which will make me feel like I have suffered a loss. I don't want to move from that place of fear. I want to move from a place of art and bravery and empathy.

Your turn. And be bold!

FIVE

SHOULD I GET AN MFA?

PART I:

As someone who not only has an MFA (Masters in Fine Arts) in Fiction, but also a Masters in Creative Writing, it may seem like I'd be biased in my opinion here. I went to school for an extra five years for two degrees with a focus on writing creatively, so I must think it's a good thing for all aspiring writers, right? The answer that I'll give you here is a bit more complicated than you might imagine, but to put it simply: it depends.

As with the other sections in this book, I'm drawing on my own personal experiences and offering you my most honest advice based on my experiences alone. I don't work for any university, so I really have no skin in the game; in other words, nobody will pay me to get you to apply to their program. My only goal here is to help someone who knows a bit less than me about writing programs know a bit more. When I applied for programs back in 2008, I knew a whole lot of nothing, and it would have been nice to have some assistance.

At the time, I was living in Spain, and while my year of teaching English, traveling, drinking Rioja, and eating copious amounts of queso Manchego was great, I knew even then that the Spanish lifestyle wasn't sustainable, at least not long term. Also, my dream wasn't to be an ESOL teacher—ultimately, I still wanted to write, to do something with creative writing. If I got into a program, I told myself, great, I'd have a few years to work on my writing in earnest. And if I didn't, I'd be fine living in a country where I could work part time and still have enough money for rent, groceries, and travel while I figured out my next steps.

I applied to the University of Iowa Writers' Workshop (only because it was and still is considered to be 'the best' and I put that in quotations because what is considered good writing is subjective and depends on who you read and who is in your literary cannon), the University of California at Irvine because Michael Chabon worked there (I loved *The Amazing Adventures of Kavalier & Clay*) and both the MFA and MA program at the University of Texas at Austin because I'd visited in 2007 for the South by Southwest film festival and enjoyed the city. I didn't really understand the difference between an MFA and an MA—more on this soon—and figured two shots was just better odds. I didn't care which one I got into.

I applied to these programs by the December deadlines and then forgot all about it and kept living my Spanish fantasy. Not until the rejections started coming in around March of 2009 was I reminded of my dormant writing dream. First, I was rejected from UC Irvine, then Iowa, and finally the MFA program at UT. For some reason, though, they put me on the waiting list for the MA program. I figured that getting off the wait list was a crapshoot, so again, I forgot about the whole business for a few weeks. But then, in April of 2009, I got an email saying I was formally accepted to the Creative Writing department at UT Austin, and would be fully funded for two years, if I still wished to accept. I accepted.

Before I move on, I want to return to the question of the difference between an MA and an MFA. What you need to know before deciding which program is best for you is to first know what your personal goals are. If, for example, you want to have a more formal academic education and training in literature alongside the chance to workshop nonacademic writing (though, be prepared to write quite a few lengthy research papers), then an MA in English with a concentration in Creative Writing is probably better. The MFA, on the other hand, will mostly be focused on your creative writing and taking the steps you need to complete a creative project you will hopefully publish one day, such as a novel, short story collection, or book of poems.

Both the MA and MFA should qualify you to teach Composition or Creative Writing at the university level (though this depends on the city, state, and school, really, so do your research) and secondary schools, but the MA tends to offer more pedagogy and more variety in what you teach. You might teach Composition, but you also might act as a Teaching Assistant for American, British, or World Literature classes. If you ultimately want to teach, make sure you investigate the course offerings and curriculum of the program you are applying to; some provide in-depth training for teachers, while others pretty much throw you into the classroom. All of this requires a bit of research on your part, but to distill the difference down to the essentials: an MA in Creative Writing offers more options for those who also want to study and analyze literature and learn how to teach it, and an MFA will be more focused on becoming a published author of creative work (not academic or research papers).

As someone who has both an MA and MFA, I can offer insight into two very specific programs. Again, not all schools are the same, so be sure to do your research and talk to alums, if possible. The first piece of advice I would give to the younger writers out there: don't go straight into an MA or MFA from undergrad. I took a year off from school to work (although working in Spain was minimal stress, not gonna lie) but it was invaluable for giving me experiences, and those experiences were important sources for creativity and stories. If you haven't really lived, what are you going to write about?

Of course, some people have lived a lot by twenty-two, perhaps more than the average person. Still, if you can, don't rush the process. Young talent needs time to mature, to understand what the gift of time and space to write really means. It's rare—near impossible, really—to be gifted two or three years where your only job is to read and write. So why not do it when you know you'll make the most of it? Of course, there are the rare people who know without a shadow of a doubt that they want to write, who know what the gift is, and for those of you like that, far be it from me to tell you what to do.

In my case, I started my MA at twenty-three, and to be honest, I think I was too young. I didn't have a handle on my voice, didn't know what I wanted to write about, didn't have confidence, discipline, or a solid writing routine. What I had was a lot of anxiety and freak outs about my talent and imposter syndrome. I was accepted to UT, sure, but on the waiting list. I was an alternate. I felt like I had to prove my worth, and half the time, I doubted it, which made for a not so fun first semester.

The other difficult part of the program at UT, at least at the time, was the lack of training us first years were given in terms of pedagogy. We got to choose what genre we'd like to TA for (World, American, British), and the professors I worked with were brilliant and lovely, but there were no classes on how to teach, no tips for classroom management, best practices for grading, etc. We just did it, and I did it with a lot of upset stomachs.

Coming into the program, I'd thought that when I graduated, I could teach full time and write on the side. But after seeing how much work it was just to be a TA, I had my doubts. The good news is that in exchange for TAing, I received free tuition and a small stipend, which meant that I didn't pay anything for grad school, ever. During the summers I had to work, but at the time it wasn't too expensive to live in Austin and I found plenty of gigs. (And by the way, there are many programs out there that have funding like this, so if you can, don't pay a penny for a writing degree.) And while I learned a lot about teaching on the ground, I think more training would have helped me and others like me with no real teaching experience. I also think being older would have given me more confidence to know that I didn't need to worry so much.

The best part for me of the MA program, outside of my cohort and professors, was the last semester. This is because we didn't have to teach or take literature classes—all we needed was to take a workshop, write, and submit a creative thesis. That last semester was when I felt most in tune with my talent, drive, and discipline. It took over a year to get there…and then I graduated. I was a Master in Creative Writing, with about 100 pages of a first novel written. I'd submitted the first chapter to a story contest held by *The Austin Chronicle*, and won second place and some cash. I'd also won the MA thesis award, and had words of encouragement from my peers, as well as my thesis advisor, Elizabeth McCracken, who was kind as well as being a gifted writer and teacher. At twenty-five, I had a lot going for me when it came to writing.

Unfortunately, when I graduated in 2011, it also coincided with the recession. I applied for teaching jobs and didn't even get called in for interviews, partly because the MA wasn't a terminal degree (meaning it wasn't the highest academic degree given in Creative Writing—that would be the MFA). An MA in Creative Writing, I now understood, was more of a stepping-stone to a PhD in English, and the idea of spending at least three more years in graduate school studying literature and not writing, just when I'd hit my stride, was out of the question. (It's important to note, too, that at this time, it wasn't common practice to get a PhD in Creative Writing; also, I didn't even know that was an option.)

In 2011 there were too many people with degrees who wanted the same jobs as I did, and between an MA or an MFA in Creative Writing, the universities preferred to hire the MFAs, or the ones with books already published. Left with few options, I turned, instead, to writing in a different context. I worked as a freelancer, writing SEO content, and then as a copy editor for an educational publishing house. After a few months of this, I lost any drive I had because all I could focus on was how to pay my rent. I did have a safety net—I could have moved back in with my parents—but I didn't want to leave Austin. In the end, I felt as if I had gone to school for nothing but a fancy piece of paper.

So, I did what a lot of writers do: I stopped writing.

PART II:

What I did after getting my MA will not be talked about here (wait for the memoir) but suffice it to say that while I didn't completely stop writing, I did lose any discipline instilled in me during grad school. I wrote only when I felt like it, took notes down for stories, and usually forgot to follow through. I wrote conservation focused blogs, book reviews for *The Miami Herald,* and short articles on the food and literary scene for the *Miami New Times.*

I wouldn't write again in any serious way until 2014, nearly four years after I received my MA. That year I was working as an editor at a local publishing company in Miami, which produced tour guides and on-board lifestyle magazines for cruise ships. I wasn't unhappy per se, but I was bored and uninspired. I had all the things we're supposed to want in this country—benefits, a 401k, healthcare, a growing salary—and while I did want those things for safety and comfort, something kept needling its way into my head. Something that told me it would be a shame to give up on my dream. That it wasn't too late to try again.

As I mentioned in the intro, I applied to only two MFA programs and got into UM. By the time I started my program, I was twenty-nine and in a far different place in terms of talent and temperament than I was at twenty-three. I'd lived in different countries, had many jobs, and knew that every year that passed meant it was going to be harder for me to write full time. I appreciated what had been offered to me and I knew going into it that I wanted to leave with a full draft of a book. I didn't know what that book was about, but I knew I would find it. I also knew that I would take advantage of every opportunity: every author event, craft talk, festival, and extra workshop. And lastly, I knew I had to cut out a lot of the unhealthy things I was doing, namely too much partying, which is easy to do in Miami.

Like the MA, my MFA program was fully funded; the way this worked is that during our first year, we worked ten hours at the writing center tutoring UM students and faculty members. Then, during our second year, we would teach Composition and Creative Writing courses. If we stayed for the third year, we taught but did not have to take any classes. In my three years, I wrote in a way that I hadn't before. I treated my time with reverence and respect, and worked through countless drafts of stories, poems, and finally, my first novel. I went to all the talks, spoke with authors and agents and publishers, made friends with my cohort, broke up with my cohort, but never strayed from the writing path. I had wonderful professors and mentors, and it worked for me. It changed my life.

If you want to focus on your creative writing, then I think getting an MFA is the way to go. My only advice is to research who you will be working with and see if you can envision yourself learning from them, and to be honest about whether you're okay with taking some required courses that are not writing related. I would also strongly suggest, again, that you don't pay for an MFA, as the odds of making a lot of money as a writer are slim. Plus, there are plenty of programs that will pay you, either in grants and scholarships or instructor positions. There's no need to go into debt over writing and doing so is setting you up for more difficulty than it's worth, in my opinion.

To reiterate: determine what's important to you in a program first, then do your research. Be prepared to make sacrifices and use the time you get in either program to your advantage. If you don't make friends, it doesn't matter. You're there for your art. Time and money to write is never guaranteed, so if you get it, run like hell with it.

DE GREFF DOOR #5

"Certainly for artists of all stripes, the unknown, the idea
or the form or the tale that has not yet arrived is
what must be found. It is the job of artists to open doors
and invite in prophesies, the unknown, the unfamiliar."
—Rebecca Solnit, *A Field Guide to Getting Lost*

In the spirit of exploration and discovery, journal on, or start a new poem/scene/or story or essay about a time that you confronted the unknown or unfamiliar. This can be based on your own life, or you can make it up. Either way, lean into the process and open that door to what must be found.

SIX

WHAT TO DO WITH YOUR WRITING

THIS SECTION WILL not apply to you if your goals for writing do not go beyond writing for yourself. That's okay, really, and I'm not one to judge, but for me—and probably for you, too, if you're reading this book, even if you're not ready to admit it yet—writing is meant to be shared. Remember that feeling you got the first time you read a book that made you feel less alone? I think that's the main reason we do what we do: to connect with others, to feel like we have an audience somewhere, and not for the ego (though yes, there is a bit of ego involved, and for some people a bit too much in my opinion) but for the bridge we create from one person to another, from writer to reader. Perhaps that's a bit utopian for some of you, but it's what keeps me going during the hard times.

Once you have decided that you want to be a writer, the first step is to write, obviously. But there's more to it than that—you need to share it. That means letting your writing go at some point and sending it to someone you trust. But how do I know when I'm ready to let it go, you may be asking. I'd say usually after draft two or three, when the piece can really use another set of eyes. Don't subject anyone to a first draft unless you edit as you write, which I don't recommend, as the danger is that you'll never finish, or you'll give it up halfway through.

Take some time to let the piece breathe after the first draft is done (a few days if it's a poem, maybe a week, and the same goes for a story or an essay, but if it's a book, then I'd give it a few weeks or a month) so you can look at draft two with fresh eyes. Draft two is for cleaning the writing up, shaping it, and trimming where it needs to be trimmed, expanding where it needs to be expanded. The second draft may be more difficult than the first, especially for novels if you didn't use an outline. What I've found helpful, even if I did have an outline, is to go back through draft one before starting draft two to write out everything that happens in a bullet point list, highlighting the major events. You can create a new doc for that or grab a new notebook and title it DRAFT TWO. This will help keep you organized with names, years, plot points, etc.

From there, you can start the new draft. A word to the wise: it's easy to get overwhelmed with how to make draft two coherent and neat. You may get a clean and readable draft two if you work slowly and meticulously, but it also may not happen until draft three. Just try and be okay with however long it takes, whether you are working on a novel, memoir, short story, or poem. The only thing you'll achieve by rushing the process is having writing that you're not proud of, that isn't the best you could do, or doesn't accurately convey what you wanted it to.

Now, let's suppose you have cleaned up your writing and it is readable, free of grammar and spelling issues, and you know you need help. This is the time to let it go. And this is when you need to choose your reader (s) wisely. If you studied creative writing in school, chances are you have at least one classmate or professor that you can reach out to for help. With a peer, it's common courtesy to offer to swap writing, so if you read theirs, they read yours. With a professor, you don't have to do that, but it's likely that they just won't have the time to give a long manuscript the attention you need; still, it can't hurt to ask. If you don't have any former classmates or professors to turn to, then the next place to look for readers is in writing groups. Again, offer to swap work, and see what happens.

If you have no writing friends or acquaintances, then you should push yourself to get some. Or, if not writers, then at least readers. You'll want people to read your writing who like to read. You'll also want people who can give you constructive feedback. Comments like "I loved it," "you're so talented," and "I wouldn't change a thing," are flattering, but also, troubling. Anyone who doesn't need to change something on a second draft is a genius. (Maybe you are, but odds are low.)

Feedback should be pointed and specific, and help you get your work to where you want it to go. If you must explain aspects of your writing, then you need to keep working on it. My best advice for a reader is to find someone who reads a lot and writes a lot, because they will understand the nuances of craft and how to help you. If people say something works or doesn't work, that's okay, but if they can't verbalize the why, it will be hard to grow and progress as a writer. They should also be kind. Meanness is not a great path to art.

Of course, self-editing is important, too. And you get better at that by reading as much as possible from both estab-lished and emerging writers. Take note of why authors make the choices they do, and practice breaking it down for yourself. This will help you do it on your own.

DE GREFF DOOR #6

The following is a questionnaire to help you do more with your writing, grow as a writer, reader, and editor, and, hopefully, find your own writing community:

1. What is your current writing schedule? (Days, times, and for how long.)

2. If you don't have any schedule, or nothing very concrete, what can you commit to doing (or at least trying to do) in terms of a writing schedule over the next week?

3. Where do you think you do your best writing? Why?

4. If you don't have a writing altar yet, can you commit to making one this week? What will that look like? (You can use objects you already have like candles,

crystals, photos, plants, charms, etc., or write yourself an encouraging note, or a quote from an author you love.) Having an altar (and this does not have to be linked to religion in any way) is a concrete way to show your writing and writing life respect, care, and love. And it serves as a daily reminder for why you show up to the page again and again.

5. Do you have a stack of model texts and/or inspirational texts near your writing area? For example, if you're writing a memoir, you might have three examples of ones you love, maybe a poetry book, maybe some essays, any work you can turn to when you feel stuck, and which causes some sort of artistic joy and creation. List that stack here, aim for 5 books, and if you have none, check out Chapter Nine for some of my favorites.

6. Do you have a reader or group of readers? Why do you trust them with your writing? If you don't have readers, where can you find some? Who can you ask? (If you don't know, try starting with Meetup.com or www. pw.org/literary_places.) or join my Writing Circle at danadegreff.com

SEVEN

A PRACTICAL GUIDE TO GETTING PUBLISHED

THE FIRST THING to know before trying to get published is that you should not submit your work anywhere if your writing is not finished. Some may think that's simplistic and obvious, but you'd be surprised at how many beginning writers submit their work before it's had a proper read through or sharing it with someone else (yours truly included). Some of us are in such a rush to get published, in such a rush to have our work out there, we will submit anything to anywhere. The truth is, it's not that hard to get published. If you don't have a *Submittable* account (this is where most journals accept submissions these days) then sign up for one (it's free) and you'll soon see that there are so many literary journals and magazines in existence, the real question is how often you're willing to submit and how much you want to/can pay.

More on that soon.

To my original point, before you get published, it's a good idea to make sure the piece is done. Meaning, you have worked on it a bunch, had someone else read and offer feedback on it, and you're proud of it. This is important because while writing shit for yourself and in the process of writing toward a great piece is necessary, do you want the world to read a shitty version of your writing? I'm guessing not. You want them to read the best writing you have in you. This is also important when it comes to submission (reading) fees. Yes, some outlets don't charge submission fees, but the going rate these days for online submissions is between $3-5 for a regular submission, and an average of $20 for competitions. So, think wisely about how much money you want to invest in a piece you know could be better.

Perhaps after reading this section, you have realized that, yes, yes I do need to work on this writing thing more. But I need more of a push. I need more than just sitting in my room or a coffee shop writing. In that case, I'd suggest you consider the following options: conferences, workshops, and residencies.

The great thing about being a writer today is that there are more options than ever when it comes to offerings for growth. The best place to start is *Poets & Writers* (pw.org), which has an online database with hundreds of options to browse through. If you want to schmooze with other writers and hear interesting talks and lectures, then a conference is the way to go. If you want to have other writers read your work and provide feedback, then you'll want a workshop. If you need time and space to write, apply for residencies. And while some of these options are quite pricey, there are often work-study slots, scholarships, and grants.

The following is a list of a few programs that I have been to over the past few years that I highly recommend, but this in no way an exhaustive list.

1. **TENT Creative Writing:**

"Tent: Creative Writing welcomes aspiring and practicing writers in their twenties and thirties to the Yiddish Book Center in Amherst, Massachusetts, to workshop, read, and talk about craft and literary history. The program offers workshops on fiction, poetry, and creative nonfiction, taught by authors such as Sam Lipstye, Lisa Olstein, and Eileen Pollack."

While Tent is focused on Jewish culture and studies, you don't have to be Jewish to attend. The workshop, room and board, and most meals are covered; all you must do is get to Amherst, Massachusetts. There are morning lectures and afternoon workshops, and the cohort tends to be both small and accomplished.

2. **Key West Literary Seminar:**

"Key West Literary Seminar welcomes readers and writers to this subtropical island city. Our flagship program is the annual Seminar, a four-day event that explores a unique literary theme each January, where readers from around the world enjoy presentations by some of the best writers of our time. In our Writers' Workshop Program, also in January, writers of all levels meet in small groups with esteemed faculty to share their work and explore the craft of writing."

I've done both the seminar and workshop, and both are excellent. If you want to work on your writing, apply for the workshop early, as they offer scholarships and financial aid on a limited basis.

3. **The Lemon Tree House Residency:**

"The Lemon Tree House is an artist residency program designed to encourage the creative, intellectual and personal growth of emerging and established artists, musicians and writers in beautiful Tuscany. Its aim is to support creative process in a unique and historically rich environment, allowing devoted time, dialogue and space for creative work, as well as providing interesting opportunities for cultural exchange and development. Writers and artists have the best of both worlds-the freedom to work in peace during the day, with the option to meet up with the group for cocktails, dinner and artist talks with featured Artists and Writers-in-Residence in the evening. Located in a tranquil hamlet in the Cetona foothills, residents have access to the full grounds, as well as a workspace in their private rooms."

This is an amazing program where your only obligation is to write, and you get daily cocktail hours and homecooked dinners. Small, intimate, and a gorgeous two weeks in Italy with other writers, artists, and musicians…it's a tough residency not to love. It is a bit pricey, but you can inquire for possible work study options. And if that's not available, you can always try crowdsourcing. You'd be surprised at how many people out there love you.

4. Tin House Workshops and Residencies:

"Publisher of award-winning books of literary fiction, nonfiction, and poetry; home to a renowned workshop and seminar series; and partner of a critically acclaimed podcast, Tin House champions writing that is artful, dynamic, and original. We are proud to publish and promote writers who speak to a wide range of experience, and lend context and nuance to their examination of our world."

Tin House holds both winter and summer workshops at Reed College near Portland, Oregon, and has a variety of writers to work with as well as readings and possibilities to meet with agents and publishers one-on-one. They offer classes in poetry, fiction, YA, novel-writing and more. Most participants stay in Reed College, which isn't the most comfortable of lodgings, but the faculty is worth it. There are also residencies for parents, first books, and more.

5. Association of Writers & Writing Programs (AWP)

"The AWP Conference & Bookfair is the annual destination for writers, teachers, students, editors, and publishers of contemporary creative writing. It includes thousands of attendees, hundreds of events and bookfair exhibitors, and four days of essential literary conversation and celebration."

This conference in March offers panels, readings, lectures, and many, many opportunities to schmooze and buy books. Each year the city location changes, so be on the lookout for where they will go next (2022 is in Philadelphia). AWP isn't great for getting any writing done, but you can learn about all the programs, get inspiration, and make potential contacts in the literary world. It can be overwhelming the first time around, so my best advice is to pace yourself and take lots of breaks.

Okay, let's say that *now* you have a finished piece, and it's ready to go and you want to try and get it published. The question is, where to submit? The best way to get that answer for yourself is to think about the publications you like to read and where you think your writing would be a good fit. (And if you don't read any literary journals or magazines, then you got some more work to do.)

It may help to think of submitting writing like a job interview: would you go to the interview without knowing anything about the company? Probably not, because then they would see that you didn't care about them, so why should they care about you? If you don't know where to start, I'd look for outlets that publish work like yours, or ones you admire. This can be done with a quick google search, or by visiting *Poets and Writers*, or *Submittable*. Choose about 5 to start with and try and pick out what they publish and why.

Here are some of my long-term faves in no particular order to get you started if you're starting from scratch:

1. *Brevity*

2. *The Sun Magazine*

3. *Orion Magazine*

4. *One Story*

5. *The Rumpus*

When you feel like you have your research down, then, as I mentioned earlier, you'll need a *Submittable* account to send out your work. Back in the day, you'd have to mail your submissions (on paper!) to the magazines and journals who would then send you a SASE (Self Addressed Stamped Envelope!) to tell you if they were going to publish you or not.

Shockingly, some places still do this (I'm looking at you, *Paris Review*) but most now work only through *Submittable*, which is an online platform that allows you to upload and submit your writing to hundreds, nay, thousands of outlets. I suggest submitting a piece to no more than ten places at a time, for your wallet, yes, and because it's a nice clean number.

Side note: back in the day, magazines also took umbrage with simultaneous submissions, but these days everyone does it. You can submit your piece to many places all at once, just let them know if it is accepted for publication elsewhere.

After you're done submitting your first round of work, congratulate yourself. You took one of the hardest steps of being a writer, which is sharing your writing and opening yourself up to rejection. More on that in the next chapter, but for now, take a moment to celebrate your journey as a writer so far. If you've made it to this point in the book, odds are you've figured out that this is a damn hard thing to do, and it's an ebb and flow. We have off days, on days, and everything in between, but if you keep showing up, keep believing in your writing, then you absolutely have more stamina than most. Go get yourself a bottle of wine, some ice cream, a bubble bath, or all three. You deserve it.

Now, for those of you who are working on longer projects such as a novel, memoir, YA book, children's book, etc., you may also be interested in finding an agent. For that, you'll need a query letter. The first thing to know about writing a query letter is that it is super important that you make sure your book is done BEFORE you send out queries to agents. Why? If it's not done, and you send them pages and then they ask for the whole manuscript and you need to backtrack, they'll most likely not want to read the book anymore. That means you lost your chance with them, and you look like an amateur, and nobody wants that.

So. First finish the book. Make it as clean, tight, and fabulous as possible. Then, write an elevator pitch. This is a short synopsis of the book, usually no more than a paragraph or two. Be as succinct as possible, and if you don't know how to write this, look at the books on your shelves. The jacket copy, which is the description inside the book (or sometimes on the back) is the synopsis. It sells the story, and that's what you need to do for your own book.

Next, you'll want to put in some info about yourself. Again, this should not be too long, maybe a paragraph. Let the agent know a bit about you, and if you have any writing achievements. If you don't, it's okay. A lot of agents are excited by talented writers who seem to come from nowhere. Just let them get a sense of who you are without being too modest or braggadocios. Once you have your book description down pat and a nice bio, you'll want to go back to the top, which is the greeting and opening of the query. This is where you let the agent know that you know who they are, who they've worked with, and what they like. And how do you do this? Allow me to introduce you to *The Poets and Writers* Literary Agents Database: https://www.pw.org/literary_agents

There are hundreds of agents listed here, and you'll need to spend a few hours, at least, combing through and looking for what makes sense for your book. You can filter by theme, depending on what you're writing, and it's great because not only do agents list what they are interested in representing, they also show who they currently represent.

Finding an agent is, weirdly, like finding a romantic partner. You want to have shared interests, and you want to start off on the right foot. If you're a fiction writer, for example, you wouldn't query an agent who specializes in memoir only. If you write children's books, reaching out to an agent who works on romance novels is silly. Spend a good amount of time on this, take notes, and then, in your intro, include a line or two that points to why you chose them. Everyone likes a compliment, and agents are no different. If you think they have good taste, they will be more inclined to listen to you and read your excerpt.

A note on excerpts: how many pages you send depends on each agent. Read their bios on their pages at the publishing house they work at to know. Some want 10 pages, for example, and some want the first chapter. It varies. The final element for the query letter is the closing words, which should be succinct (see a pattern here?) and polite, and not pushy or desperate. If they want to get back to you, they will. I suggest sending out ten letters at a time. Which leads me to what happens after you send those query letters...

First, be patient. Do not send a follow up email, unless it has been months since you've heard from them. This is a sure-fire way to not get your pages read. If the agent wants to read more of your work, they will ask for the full manuscript. If they don't, they will send you a pass. Usually this is a standard email, maybe even automated, though sometimes it may be a nice rejection with feedback. Next, be kind to yourself and don't get discouraged if it doesn't happen right away. All it takes is one yes. Corny, but true.

DE GREFF DOOR #7

Journal on the following: What is your ultimate goal when it comes to writing? Don't hold yourself back here. If the goal is to publish and start your own publishing house, write that down. If the goal is to have an HBO miniseries made from your book, with you as the star, write that down. There is no limit when it comes to dreaming!

EIGHT

HOW TO DEAL WITH REJECTION

JUST LIKE DEATH and taxes, rejection is inevitable in life, so it should come as no surprise that if you write and submit your writing for publication, grants, scholarships, and writing programs, you're going to face a lot of rejection, and hear a lot of nos. To know this does not make the sting any less painful, of course, and I won't lie and say it doesn't still hurt me, even after submitting work for more than a decade. It's your work, after all, and it comes from you, so it makes sense that you would take a no personally, at least on some level.

Much like it's a good idea to get comfortable with the idea of writing shitty first drafts, it's the same for rejection letters. They will come and you can't let them stop you from writing or trying to publish. There is a plethora of anecdotes about famous writers you love who got rejected many times, of writers who wanted to quit, or writers who threw whole drafts away. Please don't give up, don't quit, and don't ever throw any work away! What you think is shit today may turn out to be gold in ten years. (Also, what one person doesn't like another may love. Taste is subjective.) The reality is, if you want to get published, this is part of the process. It may sound harsh, but it's also a bit of a numbers game. The more you submit, the more chances you have to be published or accepted into a program, of which there are plenty.

I will say that in the beginning of my writing career I made all the classic mistakes because I didn't know any better. I'm going to share them here because I don't want you to do the same thing I did, and also because I believe writing should be more of communal process. We don't have to hold our mistakes or joys so close to our hearts—the more we share, the better literary citizens we become.

Hence, I give you my top 12 early writing blunders:

1. Writing one draft of anything and thinking it was done (oh, baby Dana);

2. Not showing anyone my work before I submitted it to a magazine, contest, or residency;

3. Submitting to literary mags I didn't read;

4. Spending a great deal (20 bucks a pop, usually) submitting to writing contests with work that wasn't a good fit;

5. Not reading formatting or guidelines for submissions closely;

6. Not reading my work out loud;

7. Not including cover letters;

8. Believing that I could only write what I "know;"

9. Taking workshop comments too seriously, especially those from other writers who were unnecessarily negative or personal in their critiques;

10. Believing that rejections meant my writing sucked and I sucked;

11. Not counting positive feedback from editors in rejection letters as wins. (They are! They took the time to write to you and that's huge, especially since they normally receive hundreds, if not thousands of submissions.);

12. Not asking other writers for help. Oftentimes, especially if you take a class from someone, they'll be willing to give you some advice. Don't be pushy or aggressive, but humble and grateful, and you'll be

surprised at how much people will help answer your writing and publishing questions.

Hopefully you don't make the same blunders as I did, but if you do (or already did) know that it's okay. We're not perfect, right? But once you know, you can at least try and do better next time.

DE GREFF DOOR #8

THE FOLLOWING IS something I did a few years ago that was helpful and cathartic. I had just accepted the fact that my first novel would not be published unless I did some serious reworks and rewriting, after already having reworked it and rewrote it for nearly four years. It was a difficult few days, a period in which I cried, vented to my closest friends, and took copious walks. There was no answer or solution to change the reality of my situation. The book had already been sent out to 20+ editors.

And after so many nos (many of them quite nice, but a nice no in this situation felt just as shitty) and a maybe, contingent on a major rework that resulted in another no, I was seriously ready to give up. I'd quit my cushy job to get an MFA, gone to many residencies, been published, and been told my work was great, that I was talented, and that there was no doubt

I would succeed and now I was most definitely failing. Who was I to talk about writing without a damn book?

Perhaps somewhat paradoxically, I don't believe you need to be published to be a writer. If you write, then you can call yourself a writer. But for me and my goals—to connect with people, bring attention to underrepresented voices and mental health, contribute to the nature writing cannon—being published was nonnegotiable. I felt like a fraud, and for many days I didn't write and didn't talk to anyone about it. I read a lot, and I knew for a fact that there were really shitty books being published, and, perhaps even worse, some of those shitty books had landed the authors six-figure deals. Maybe I just wasn't meant to be a writer, I thought.

Then, a week or two later, I got the idea to write myself a letter. I don't know why that came up, but perhaps it was inspired by a practice I'd started a year or two earlier of writing letters to myself when in was in a low place. Instead of being harsh or mean, I tried to be kind and understanding. (A tall order when you are in the throes of self-doubt, to be sure, but it couldn't hurt.) And the thing is, after I wrote this two-page letter and put it in an envelope onto which I wrote "for when you want to give up" I did feel better.

I took the time to listen to myself, to validate myself, and let it go, more or less. It still was disappointing, it still hurt, but the letter allowed me to shift to the future rather than stay in the past. Maybe this book didn't work, but the next one could. Maybe it just wasn't meant to be my first book. Maybe that book would help me write the next one. This was meant to be a lifelong career, so what did a few years matter in the grand scheme of life?

Two years later, I've only looked at the letter once. And I'm still writing. Your challenge is to write yourself a letter like this, for when you want to give up, to remind yourself to keep going.

NINE

RECOMMENDED READING

REMEMBER HOW I said in the last chapter that you don't need to publish to be a writer? Well, that's true, however, you do need to read, and for me that's non-negotiable. If someone tells me they're a writer and I ask them what they're reading and they say nothing, or that the last book they read was a year ago…I stop listening. To choose not to read is lazy and hypo-critical if you're a writer. What swimmer doesn't swim? What film director doesn't watch movies? What chef doesn't taste new foods? It just doesn't make sense.

However, if you're not reading due to a case of not know-ing what to read or where to start when it comes to books, I got you. I suggest you start by reading what you love, and then read outside of your chosen genre so that you can learn and be inspired by those who don't write like you. Also, reading what you don't love can be helpful, because to know why you don't like something is to know why or how not to do it yourself. Reading outside of our taste and genre pushes us to be more creative, and ultimately, better writers.

The following is, as ever, not an exhaustive list, but some of my sacred texts that I return to again and again and will hopefully inspire you, bring you joy, and act as a domino effect into other books. These are books that inspire me, move me, challenge me, and have led me to branch out in my writing and writing life. (Also, when in doubt about what to read next, look up what your favorite authors read. And then go get those books! It's a great excuse to support your local bookstores and/ or libraries.)

Fiction:

1. *Everything I Never Told You*, Celeste Ng

2. *Beloved*, Toni Morrison

3. *The Overstory*, Richard Powers

4. *The Buddha in the Attic*, Julie Otsuka

5. *Open City*, Teju Cole

6. *Kindred*, Octavia E. Butler

7. *On Earth We're Briefly Gorgeous*, Ocean Vuong

Poetry:

1. *When My Brother Was an Aztec*, Natalie Diaz

2. *Olio*, Tyehimba Jess

3. *Citizen: An American Lyric*, Claudia Rankine

4. *Night Sky with Exit Wounds*, Ocean Vuong

5. *Autobiography of Red*, Anne Carson

Memoir:

1. *The Chronology of Water*, Lidia Yuknavitch

2. *Dear Senthuran: A Black Spirit Memoir*, Akwaeke Emezi

3. *In the Dream House*, Carmen Maria Machado

4. *H Is for Hawk*, Helen Macdonald

5. *Hunger: A Memoir of (My) Body*, Roxane Gay

6. *The Yellow House*, Sarah M. Broom

7. *The Periodic Table,* Primo Levi

Short Stories:

1. *Drinking Coffee Elsewhere*, ZZ Packer

2. *Last Evenings on Earth*, Roberto Bolaño

3. *Her Body and Other Parties*, Carmen Maria Machado

4. *After the Quake*, Haruki Murakami

5. *Friday Black*, Nana Kwame Adjei-Brenyah

Hybrid:

1. *The People of Paper*, Salvador Plascencia

2. *Bluets*, Maggie Nelson

3. *Good Talk: A Memoir in Conversations*, Mira Jacob

4. *Dictee*, Theresa Hak Kyung Cha

5. *Journey to Armenia*, Osip Mandelstam

Nonfiction/Essays:

1. *Braiding Sweetgrass: Indigenous Wisdom, Scientific Knowledge, and the Teachings of Plants*, Robin Wall Kimmerer

2. *How to Write an Autobiographical Novel*, Alexander Chee

3. *All About Love*, bell hooks

4. *The Book of Delights*, Ross Gay

5. *Dear Friend, from My Life I Write to You in Your Life*, Yiyun Li

6. *A Field Guide to Getting Lost*, Rebecca Solnit

YA:

1. *Juliet Takes a Breath*, Gabby Rivera

2. *Felix Ever After*, Kacen Callender

3. *The Hate U Give*, Angie Thomas

4. *The Outsiders*, S.E. Hinton

5. *The Perks of Being a Wallflower*, Stephen Chbosky

TEN

49 OPEN DOORS

OVER THE PAST few years of teaching creative writing classes in various genres to thousands of students of all ages, backgrounds, and skill levels, I've become quite good at coming up with ways to get people writing creatively, or at least to get rid of the pesky blank page. These prompts are meant to act as openings—doors—to small and big projects, musings and questions, silly and serious issues, or to simply let go of the day and have fun.

Some of these are geared toward fiction, others poetry, nonfiction, and hybrid forms, and some are meant to get you outside, but many have no specific genre, and none of them are connected by theme or subject except to get the words flowing. A few are one-liners, and others take longer to digest. Start from the beginning, at the end, or anywhere in between.

Happy writing!

1. A character just said "I love you" to someone else for the first time. The other person doesn't say it back. Write that scene. Then write what happened leading up to that scene, and afterwards.

2. After dinner, there is a blackout across the entire city. This has never happened before. What does it feel like? Who is around? What are the smells, the sensations in the air? And how long is it dark for?

3. Describe in copious amounts of detail any moment of shame from your life. This can be your own moment, or one you observed. What did you learn from it, or what did you perceive that the other person may have learned?

4. Write at least one scene where your protagonist tries to get something they want, and they fail in the process. What are the consequences? How do they react? How do they fail?

5. Eavesdrop on at least five conversations today or over the next few days. Make a list of the most interesting/ weird/funny/sweet/ awful/ strange things you hear (go for a list of 20, if possible). Then use these for a current

or future project, either for dialogue, or an image, or a conflict, etc.

6. The sense of smell is closely linked with memory and certain smells can evoke specific and particular memories; Marcel Proust, in his *Remembrance of all Things Past*, wrote that a bite of madeleine vividly recalled childhood memories of his aunt giving him the same cake before going to mass on a Sunday.

   Write a scene in which a character (or you) smells something that takes them back in time by way of a flashback. Avoid, if you can, the words "remembers," "thought back to," and "recalled," and lean into the sense of smell.

7. If infinity is a concept describing something without any bound, something limitless, endless, and immense, what in your characters' life (or yours) can be described in the same way? This can be a concept (maybe love), or a dream they had, or how they view themselves and their potential…

8. Start a scene with the line: "and that's when the terror began."

9. Start a scene with: "I remember it this way."

10. The idea of traveling in place (or armchair travel) may have originated with Xavier de Maistre's 1794 *Voyage autour de ma chambre*, a fantasy written about a "journey around his room" in which he writes:

"When I travel through my room, I rarely follow a straight line: I go from the table towards a picture hanging in a corner; from there, I set out obliquely towards the door; but even though, when I begin, it really is my intention to go there, if I happen to meet my armchair en route, I don't think twice about it, and settle down in it without further ado."

Take a minute or two right now to look around the room you are in (ideally this should be the room in which you work, eat, or sleep normally). Try not to see it as a familiar place, but rather, as if it were an unknown destination, an undiscovered place, somewhere that will bring up unexpected memories. You are an explorer looking beyond what meets the eye, and beyond what you usually see. Be as creative as you like, perhaps writing this in the form of a poem or letter to a loved one back home, or simply as a series of 'travel notes.' Can you make the familiar feel unfamiliar?

11. Write this line down: "That summer, everybody was listening to that song. It was playing everywhere." Now, if you have internet, look up and listen to this song: "Come Meh Weh" by Sudan Archives.

    Write whatever words come to you, whatever feelings you feel, whatever you see in your mind's eye. If it helps you can close your eyes for a minute, or for the entire song. When the song is done, write a short piece of flash fiction or poetry, using whatever the song made you feel, and what you saw in your mind's eye, and where you went in your head, as the guiding inspiration.

12. Use one of the following lines to start a new scene, chapter, poem, story, book:

    -"Suitcase in hand, you head to the airport."

    -"'Just say it,'" you silently tell yourself. You knew you'd regret it if you didn't."

    -"As she checks the mail, she notices a letter that makes her heart race."

    -"The woods looked different that day."

    -"They opened the doors to the house and inside was a…"

-"She knew that if she went into the mosque, her life would change forever."

-"For a moment, he isn't sure if he heard right. But, yes, his boss really did just say that."

13. Do some research on the color red. Incorporate some of your findings into a new scene, line of dialogue, poetic image, or journal entry. (For example...did you know that red is the first color humans perceive after black and white?)

14. Choose 3-5 of your favorite words and free write on one (or all of them) for 10-15 minutes. When you finish, see if you can use the word, or the words, that came out of your free write for your current project. (For example, some of my favorite words are: jubilee, mariposa, indigo, and sassafras.)

15. Right now, either using a google search, your phone, laptop, or an actual photo in an album or on a wall, choose ONE photo that you find yourself drawn to. Begin with simple description, writing what you see in the picture. Then move beyond the visual and into the sounds, smells, and feels of that moment. If it's from your life, go into the memories that it brings up, and if it's not from your life, imagine the world beyond the

frame and pull whatever you need into your piece to tell the story of that photo.

16. In an interview on the *Between the Covers Podcast*, Natalie Diaz, Latina and Mojave American poet, said: "I do think love is a-not knowing [...]."

    Your challenge, inspired by Diaz, is to write a love poem, or an ode, to someone, something, some being, or an idea...whatever it is that moves you into a space of 'not knowing.' Maybe you do this in the epistolary (letter) form, or maybe it is a scene between two characters in your current project, or perhaps it is a sonnet to yourself, a love song of sorts.

17. Write somewhere in water—literally. Take your notebook and write in the ocean, a river, a pool, a puddle, or even your bathtub. Can you 'become' water? Describe that.

18. Write about one being from nature every day for 7 days, if possible. Think of this as a sort of "7 ways of looking at _____" exercise. Don't hold back and don't self-edit. At least not for the first draft!

19. Write the inner monologue of a native plant to your state, or the sounds of photosynthesis, or your brain in

the mountains. Write whatever you think is impossible to write, and then write some more.

20. Find a park near you (a state park, national park, or reserve, if possible, but a city park will do) and before you go, research it. When was it created and why, what was it before, who was there before, what can be found there, etc. When you visit, take notes on whatever strikes you. Afterwards, leave the notes alone for at least a day. Then start a new piece incorporating your research and findings.

21. Write a short entry using the four directions: north, east, south, and west. This can be a poem, a scene, flash fiction, or micro nonfiction, or just a stream of conscious activity.

22. Choose three quotes from anyone you find inspiring to help you finish whatever project (s) you are working on and tape them above your writing desk, or on your notebook or computer. These can be from writers, but they don't have to be.

23. Write a one-minute monologue in which you focus on a story from your childhood. This can be humorous, but it doesn't have to be. Read it out loud to yourself, or to someone else, and see if you can then rewrite it

to some sense of purpose: closure, humor, mystery, empathy, etc.

24. From Rebecca Solnit's *A Field Guide to Getting Lost*: "Certainly for artists of all stripes, the unknown, the idea or the form or the tale that has not yet arrived, is what must be found."

    Your challenge is to write a scene in which one of your character's encounters the unknown. This can be a new job, a difficult emotion, a trail, a date...get creative with it and do not fear the unfamiliar!

25. Choose an element from the periodic table. Do research on it for 10-15 minutes, then incorporate your findings into a scene of dialogue between three or more characters.

26. Write a new scene which starts with one of the following lines:

    -"Coded messages were only the beginning."

    -"Night was when noises began, ones she couldn't forget, no matter how hard she tried."

    -"The _____ had the smell of danger. It smelled like this:"

27. Choose one of the following words: amber, Iceland, prism, undocumented, spruce, then research its etymology. With your findings, write a poem, or a series of poems on the word. These don't have to be sensical.

28. Make a list of 10-20 things from one of your current story/novel/poem/essay's settings (props, if you will) that can serve as a portrait of one of your characters. In other words, think about how setting informs character and vice versa.

29. Google the podcast "The Source of Creativity" from the *Ted Radio Hour*, which is all about creativity and inspiration. If you have heard it before, no matter, listen to it again. Each time I listen to it, I get new ideas and am ready to tackle any writing project I'm working on, or inspired to begin a fresh new piece. Once you have finished, journal on the following questions:

-Where do you find inspiration?

-How do you get into the flow state?

-What new things did you learn from the podcast, and what can you incorporate into your writing life starting now?

30. Write 5-10 meditations on the word 'cold' using the website *wordnik* for assistance. To say something is cold is kinda dull, but to get to the heart of the cold can really bring a sentence, a paragraph, a scene, alive. Don't hold back in the first draft, and in the second, read it out loud and highlight the parts that make you feel the cold, that will also transmit to the reader and perhaps even inspire them to grab a mug of tea...

31. Write an ode to something ordinary in your life, or something you have previously passed over. Or, not an ode, but a letter. Or, not a letter, but a monologue. Something in which you directly address an inanimate object, and make the audience feel as if it comes alive.

32. Write a scene that focuses on the budding friendship between two of your characters or shows how they go from acquaintances to friends. What, in your words, in how you show it, makes a friendship? How can you convey to readers (maybe even without using the word 'friend') that these two people now care about each other in a real and tangible manner that will in turn get readers to care about them?

33. "Who is the Bad Art Friend" came out in *The New York Times Magazine* on October 5, 2021. Read it, if you haven't already, and/or listen to it on *The Daily*

podcast. Once you're done, write a creative piece in reaction to/inspired by either art imitating life, theft, creativity, two friends who have a falling out, or what it's like to try and sue someone. This can be based on truth...or not.

34. This week, follow author Sarah Sentilles' advice to "Be a Magpie" (#3 on her list entitled "11 Things I Wish I'd Known About Writing 11 Years Ago"). Do this in a separate doc or in your notebook and practice non-restraint when it comes to attraction/interest; collect everything that may (or may not) go into your current project.

35. Write about a time in which you encountered something/some person/ some being that was completely new to you. What was the experience like, using all the senses?

36. As you move throughout your week, take notes on the people you encounter. This can be people at work, on the street, at home, even on television. They also don't have to be encounters in person. Challenge yourself to take notes on what is said and unsaid, what sticks in your mind about the visuals of the person, any smells or sounds, or textures.

37. Inspired by Tolstoy's supposed assertion that "All great literature is one of two stories; a man goes on a journey, or a stranger comes to town," write about an encounter between one of your main characters and a stranger. But this is not just any stranger, this is someone who will jeopardize a relationship, either familial, romantic, or friendship wise.

38. What are your writing rituals? Do you make a cup of tea, light a candle, or meditate? Do you write down positive affirmations, do some yoga, or dance for 5 minutes? We need these rituals to declutter our mind, get in the writing flow state, and to help us better enjoy the process of writing, from idea generation to revision.

    If you don't have any, then your challenge is to create a set of writing rituals that you will do each time you sit down to write over the next 30 days.

39. *Gracias a la vida que me ha dado tanto / Me ha dado el sonido y el abecedario*
    —Violeta Parra, "Gracias a la vida"
    One of the best ways I've found to get in the mood for writing is to create a curated playlist. For example, right now I'm working on a memoir which is set primarily in Patagonia, Chile. I put together a list of

songs (such as "Gracias a la vida") that I first heard there, local groups that are important in the country, and artists that used lyrics that matched certain important events for me in my own life from 2012-2013, such as poet/singer/activist Violeta Parra.

Your challenge is to create your own playlist. This can be for a long project, say, a book, or perhaps for a poem or blog, or maybe just songs that make you feel calm and inspired in order to settle down at your writing desk with more ease.

40. *"I couldn't remember what life was like before I started walking."*
—Teju Cole, *Open City*
Today, you will participate in some flânerie. The idea is to take a walk, if you can, perhaps on your block, or perhaps in a new neighborhood or area. See if you can take a step back and 'participate fully through observation.' What does that look like, smell like, sound like, feel like, and heck, maybe even taste like?

41. Open a new browser, go to the Merriam Webster dictionary, and get on the Time Traveler page/function. Find the year you were born and challenge yourself to use **5-10 words** that were introduced to print that year. It doesn't have to make sense, or go anywhere

in particular, but you may be surprised to see where these words lead you.

Here's an example using words from my birth year:
She stood over the <u>Vietnamese potbellied pig</u>, the <u>French Tips</u> on her small hands chipped and filthy. This, she thought, heart pumping at a breakbeat, lips still tingling from the <u>chiltepin</u> from lunch, was an alternative country.

42. Open your photos on your phone (or if you're old school, a photo album) and choose the first photo that has pink in it somewhere. This photo will now be your jumping off point for a new piece of writing: it can be the memory surrounding the photo (real or imagined) or a new event or scene in a story, or perhaps a line of dialogue, or you can borrow the location for setting, or an interesting object as a symbol or important item to a character in a novel you're working on.

43. "It took me a long time to recognize that while I wanted to know love, I was afraid to be truly intimate."

—bell hooks, *All About Love*

How do you feel about love these days? (Or, if you prefer, how does one of your characters feel about love?) In what ways are you afraid to be intimate? This can be written in scene, or perhaps as a monologue, or an honest and open letter to yourself.

44. Write a letter to someone. Maybe it's a friend, maybe a relative, or maybe your beloved oak tree. This can also be a letter written from one character to another, or, if you're looking for a twist, perhaps a letter shows up in a new scene and it is written by someone anonymous with some scandalous information to share...

45. Reach out to a friend or family member today and ask them to provide you with a list of 5 of their favorite words (any language or a mix of languages is fine). Take those words and use them as best you can in a piece of creative writing. If you're feeling extra bold, connect even further and share your piece with them when you're done.

46. Breaking out of our patterns and habits is essential for creativity, and the following activity can lead to some delightful surprises:

    1. Grab the first book you see on your nightstand/bookshelf;

    2. Turn to page 45;

    3. Copy down the first 3 lines, but from end to beginning, i.e., in reverse. For example, I chose *Bluets* by Maggie Nelson, and here are the three lines (written

from end to beginning):

"dream a in—bluet a perhaps—flower blue little a sees who troubadour medieval a of story he tells Novalis Ofterdingen von Heinrich novel unfinished his in" / "'life real' in flower blue the see to longs he aferward" / "says he 'idea the of rid get can't I.'"

By writing the sentences backwards, the idea is to focus on language in a different way. See if you can use your new scrambled lines to start a new piece (or feel free to use mine if you like!) or maybe rearrange the words further to make it fit into a piece-in-progress, or just frolic in the beauty of words.

47. SYZYGY is defined as "the nearly straight-line con-figuration of three celestial bodies (such as the sun, moon, and earth during a solar or lunar eclipse) in a gravitational system."

Write a scene, essayette, story, or poem in which a syzygy occurs.

48. Our sense of smell is known to be one of the most powerful ways to unlock memories, to transport us in our mind, emotions, and spirit to another time and place. For example, if I smell wood burning, or yerba maté, I immediately think of Patagonia, of my

time sitting around an asado or stoking the flames of a wood burning stove while drinking rounds of maté with my friends and coworkers.

List a few scents from your past and journal on how these particular smells take you back: where do you go, how does it feel to be there, what do you see, and how can you describe those scents?

49. Think about a time in which you had to change: change location, change of heart, change minds, change an old pattern that no longer serves you. Start by writing down one line after another, each one starting with the phrase: "change is."
This list doesn't have to make sense, but by incorporating anaphora (a device that consists of repeating a sequence of words at the beginnings of lines, giving them emphasis and rhythm) you may get to some interesting images, places, or insights.

For example:

Change is the green to orange on the oak tree leaves.
Change is the smell of slash pine, wet and pulpy.
Change is what happens when you decide to breathe and breathe again.

EPILOGUE

WHAT NEXT?

THE QUESTION OF what next is the simplest part of this book: write. Write, write, write, and then write some more. Also, read. And live. All of that will help you write.

My hope is that you now have more confidence, more tools, and some new books and notebooks to get you going on your individual and lifelong writing path. I also hope that you understand that there is no one way to write, no one way to be a writer, and that the path is often (always?) winding. And no matter how or when or why you write, the words can only come from you, and only you can get them out of your head and onto the page. Paradoxically, that's the writer's greatest strength and often their greatest downfall. It all comes back to us.

In other words, nobody will check in on you, or know when you're (or when you aren't) writing. Nobody will care all that much whether you do or don't, which is why the person who matters most is you. You're the one who has to want to write, yes, but also *need* to write. It took me more than a decade to develop a solid writing practice, and many years of treating writing as an acquaintance and not a loved one. But now writing is like a sister to me, and I treat her with care, kindness, and respect. Occasionally we get in fights, but we always come back together.

So, here's to you for choosing to do the thing that brings you joy, scares you, inspires you, or perhaps all three. Here's to the writerly path. It's not always well marked, or easy, or fair, but it's a beautiful way to travel.

SOURCES

Beating Imposter Syndrome

Information referenced on Imposter Syndrome is from:

Sakulku, J. (1). The Impostor Phenomenon. The Journal of Behavioral Science, 6(1), 75-97. https://doi.org/10.14456/ ijbs.2011.6

"Conscious complaining" taken from Karla McLaren's book *The Language of Emotions: What Your Feelings Are Trying to Tell You* (Boulder, CO, Sounds True Inc, 2010).

The Maya Angelou quote came from the NY Book Editors Blog "How to Overcome Imposter Syndrome as a Writer" and can be found at https://nybookeditors.com/2018/09/ how-to-overcome-imposter-syndrome-as-a-writer/

"Embrace the suck" is from Brené Brown's *Dare to Lead* (New York: Random House, 2018).

A Practical Guide to Getting Published

TENT Creative Writing program information can be found here https://www.yiddishbookcenter.org/educational-programs/tent-encounters-jewish-culture/tent-creative-writing/faq

Key West Literary Seminar program information can be found here https://www.kwls.org/

The Lemon Tree House Residency program information can be found here https://www.thelemontreehouse.org/

Tin House Workshops and Residencies program information can be found here https://tinhouse.com/workshop/residencies/

Association of Writers & Writing Programs (AWP) program information can be found here https://www.awpwriter.org/awp_conference/registration_overview

Open Doors

#6 Info on Marcel Proust, in his *Remembrance of all Things Past* can be accessed here https://www.britannica.com/topic/In-Search-of-Lost-Time

#10 Xavier de Maistre's 1794 *Voyage autour de ma chambre* can be accessed here https://publicdomainreview.org/collection/a-journey-round-my-room-1794-1871

#11 "Come Meh Weh" by Sudan Archives can be listened to and purchased here https://sudanarchives.bandcamp.com/track/come-meh-way-2

#16 *Between the Covers Podcast Natalie Diaz : Postcolonial Love Poem : Part One* can be accessed here https://tinhouse.com/podcast/natalie-diaz-postcolonial-love-poem/

#24 The quote is taken from Rebecca Solnit's *A Field Guide to Getting Lost* (New York: Penguin, 2006).

#29 The Source of Creativity" from the Ted Radio Hour can be accessed here https://www.npr.org/programs/ted-radio-hour/351538855/the-source-of-creativity

#33 Who is the Bad Art Friend" came out in *The New York Times Magazine* and can be accessed here https://www.nytimes.com/2021/10/05/magazine/dorland-v-larson.html

#34 Sarah Sentilles' "11 Things I Wish I'd Known About Writing 11 Years Ago" can be accessed here https://www.bookpage.com/behind-the-book/26179-11-things-i-wish-id-known-about-writing-11-years-ago-nonfiction/

#37 I have read conflicting views on whether or not Tolstoy actually said this quote…but it's a good quote.

#39 "Gracias a la vida" was written and performed by Violeta Parra and can be accessed and listened to here https://www.youtube.com/watch?v=NIDD2Y9lMAA

#40 The quote is taken from Teju Cole's, *Open City* (New York: Random House, 2012)

#41 Merriam Webster's Time Traveler feature can be accessed here https://www.merriam-webster.com/time-traveler/2020

#43 the quote is from bell hooks' *All About Love* (New York: HarperCollins, 2018)

#46 Quote is from Maggie Nelson's *Bluets* (Seattle: Wave Books, 2009)

#47 SYZYGY definition found at merriam-webster.com

ACKNOWLEDGEMENTS

I'm grateful for all my muses and mentors, duendes, and ride or dies. I'm lucky to have the family I do, and especially for my parents who have gifted me their support and love along the way, all the way. Thanks also to my best bish, Beverly Tan Murray, for encouraging me to keep going since that fateful day we met at the world's worst literary reading in 2014. The torture of that was worth the gift of you. You're the best friend, editor, and human I know.

To the people who set me on the path to writing, whether they know it or not, and whether they are still with us or not. To the first author who blew my mind, Toni Morrison. To the first teacher who was a kindred spirit with superb taste, my high school English teacher, Ms. Simmons. To the University of Texas at Austin MA program for giving me a taste of what a writing life could look like, and the encouragement from

ACKNOWLEDGEMENTS

my thesis director, Elizabeth McCracken. To the University of Miami MFA program for the time and space to write, and to my mentors there, specifically Chantel Acevedo, M. Evelina Galang, and Patricia Engel.

And thank you to all the students I've had over the last 10+ years, for teaching me to be more creative, patient, and caring. This is for you, and I hope you're still writing, but if you're not, then please give this book to someone who is. Y siempre pa' lante.

DANA DE GREFF is the author of *Alterations*, winner of the Rane Arroyo Chapbook Series. She has taught Creative Writing at the University of Texas at Austin, the University of Miami, Books & Books, The Loft Literary Center, Austin Bat Cave, Writing Workshops, and Writers.com. She's the recipient of a 2021 Pushcart Prize Nomination and her work has appeared in *Cosmonauts Avenue, PANK, Origins Journal*, and *Gulf Stream Magazine*, among others. She works with emerging and established writers, helping them bring their books to life through creative tools, publishing insight, and mentorship. Find out more at *danadegreff.com*.